BURN YOUR 9-5

How Regular People *Build Wealth with Real Estate*

NO EXPERIENCE?
NO CAPITAL?
NO PROBLEM.
FOLLOW THIS
STEP-BY-STEP PLAN

LACY O'LEARY

For my husband John,
Burning together
since 2004

Table of Contents

Introduction

Welcome to *Burn your 9-5*, whether you're just starting out or looking to sharpen your skills, this guide provides actionable steps, focusing on the fundamental skills, discipline, and knowledge every investor needs to thrive.

Real estate investing can seem overwhelming with complex strategies, diverse markets, and the ever-changing economic landscape. This is more than just a technical manual, it will show you how to embrace the mindset of a successful investor: resilience, adaptability, and the drive to create value not only for yourself but for those around you.

Let this guide empower you to take confident steps toward achieving your financial goals through real estate.

REAL ESTATE INVESTING BUSINESS

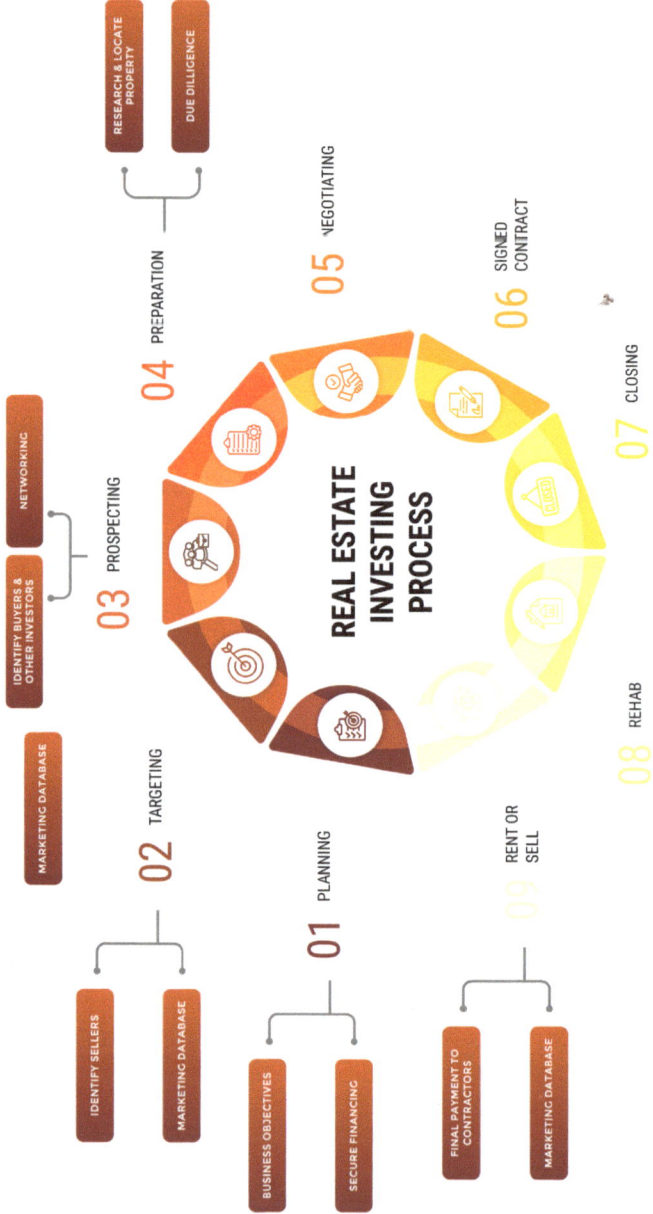

REAL ESTATE INVESTING PROCESS

01 PLANNING
- BUSINESS OBJECTIVES
- SECURE FINANCING

02 TARGETING
- IDENTIFY SELLERS
- MARKETING DATABASE

03 PROSPECTING
- IDENTIFY BUYERS & OTHER INVESTORS
- NETWORKING

04 PREPARATION
- RESEARCH & LOCATE PROPERTY
- DUE DILLIGENCE

05 NEGOTIATING

06 SIGNED CONTRACT

07 CLOSING

08 REHAB

09 RENT OR SELL
- FINAL PAYMENT TO CONTRACTORS
- MARKETING DATABASE

6

Understanding Real Estate Investing

Before you start, it's important to understand the basics. Real estate investment involves purchasing, managing, and selling property for profit.
This can include residential properties like houses and apartments, commercial properties, or even land.

Types of Real Estate Investments:

1 Residential Real Estate – Single-family homes, multi-family homes, condos, townhouses, etc.

2 Commercial Real Estate – Office buildings, retail spaces, warehouses, industrial spaces, etc.

3 REITs (Real Estate Investment Trusts) – Companies that own or finance income-producing real estate and allow investors to purchase shares.

4 Land – Investing in raw land or agricultural land for development or leasing.

5 Special purpose – Hospitality, Churches, storage, gas stations, amusement parks, etc. (properties that are uniquely designed for specific business operations or activities)

6 Mixed Use - Buildings with retail on the ground floor and apartments above, Developments combining office spaces with residential units, Communities with integrated live-work-play environments, etc.

Types of Real Estate Investments

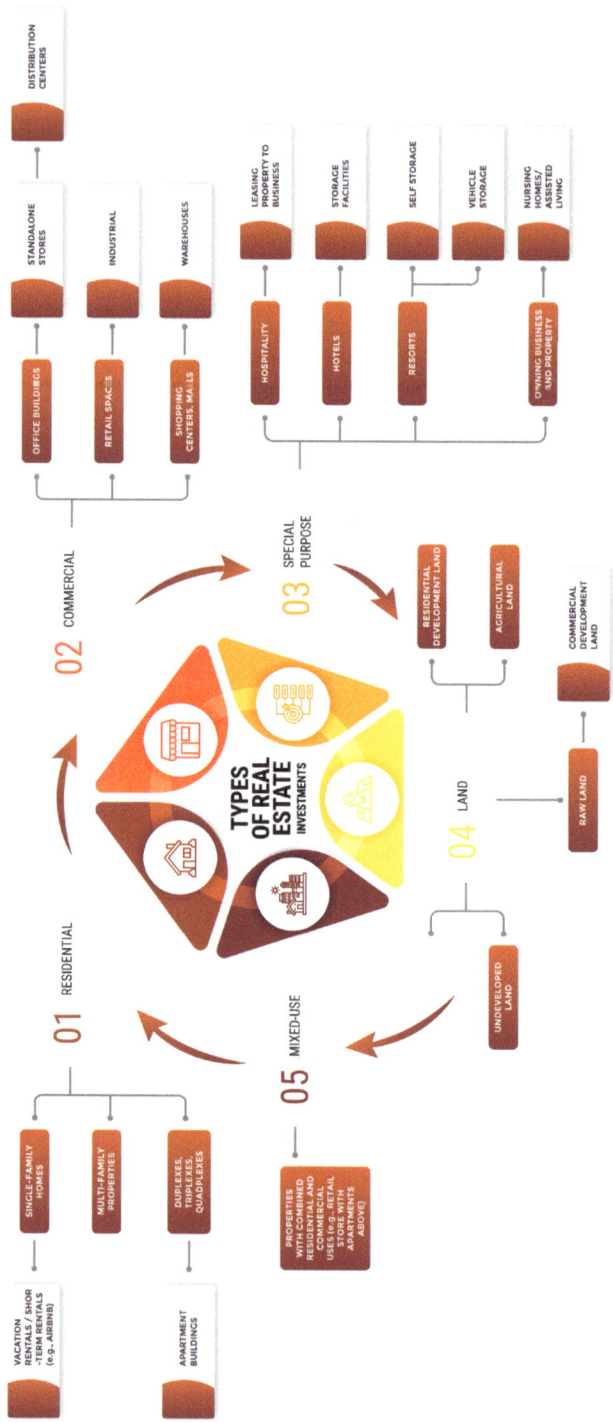

TYPES OF REAL ESTATE INVESTMENTS

01 RESIDENTIAL
- SINGLE-FAMILY HOMES
  - VACATION RENTALS / SHORT-TERM RENTALS (e.g. AIRBNB)
- MULTI-FAMILY PROPERTIES
- DUPLEXES, TRIPLEXES, QUADPLEXES
  - APARTMENT BUILDINGS

02 COMMERCIAL
- OFFICE BUILDINGS
  - STANDALONE STORES
  - DISTRIBUTION CENTERS
- RETAIL SPACES
  - INDUSTRIAL
- SHOPPING CENTERS, MALLS
  - WAREHOUSES

03 SPECIAL PURPOSE
- HOSPITALITY
  - LEASING PROPERTY TO BUSINESS
- HOTELS
  - STORAGE FACILITIES
- RESORTS
  - SELF STORAGE
  - VEHICLE STORAGE
- OWNING BUSINESS AND PROPERTY
  - NURSING HOMES / ASSISTED LIVING

04 LAND
- RESIDENTIAL DEVELOPMENT LAND
- AGRICULTURAL LAND
- COMMERCIAL DEVELOPMENT LAND
- RAW LAND
- UNDEVELOPED LAND

05 MIXED-USE
- PROPERTIES WITH COMBINED RESIDENTIAL AND COMMERCIAL USES (e.g. RETAIL STORE WITH APARTMENTS ABOVE)

CHAPTER 2

Setting
Clear Goals

Ask yourself what you are working towards.

What do you want to achieve through Real Estate? Is it cash flow, capital gains, or both?

Goals help you determine which strategies to pursue.

Examples of Goals:

> **Generate Passive Income** through rental properties.
> **Build Long-term Wealth** with appreciation of property value.
> **Diversify Investments** with different property types or REITs.
> **Achieve Financial Freedom** through consistent cash flow.

1. **Why Goals Are Essential in Real Estate Investing**

Understanding the Role of Goals in Guiding Investment Decisions

1. Goal: Generating Passive Income

> A real estate investor aiming for $5,000 monthly passive income focuses on acquiring rental properties in markets with high cash flow potential. This clarity guides them toward single-family homes or duplexes that meet their income
> requirements.
> Another investor sets a goal of acquiring 10 properties within five years. They prioritize properties that are affordable yet offer steady appreciation, ensuring consistent progress toward their target.

2. Goal: Achieving Market Diversification

> An investor decides to diversify by purchasing properties in three different states. This goal directs their research and decision-making toward regions with varying economic drivers, taking into consideration market-specific risks.

> A beginner investor seeks to invest in both residential and commercial properties. Their goals help them allocate resources wisely and seek mentorship or partnerships for commercial deals.

The Link Between Clear Goals and Long-Term Financial Success

1. Goal: Early Retirement

> A couple sets a goal to retire by age 50 with $1 million in net worth through real estate. They strategize by investing in properties with high appreciation potential and reinvesting profits from property sales to scale their portfolio.

> Another investor aims to replace their $100,000 annual salary with rental income. By breaking this goal into smaller milestones, such as acquiring one property per year, they steadily build a portfolio that supports their lifestyle.

2. Goal: Creating Generational Wealth

> A family sets a long-term goal of passing down a real estate portfolio to their children. They focus on acquiring properties in stable neighborhoods with a history of steady value appreciation.

> An investor who wants to create a legacy establishes a goal of donating a portion of their profits to community housing projects. Their focus on impact investing helps achieve both personal and philanthropic success.

Examples of Investors Who Achieved Successby Setting Actionable Goals

1. Investor Example:Brandon Turner

> Brandon Turner, a real estate investor and host of the BiggerPockets podcast, set a clear goal of achieving financial
> independence through small multifamily properties. By systematically acquiring and managing properties, he created substantial passive income and now teaches others to do the same.

2. Investor Example: Barbara Corcoran

Barbara Corcoran, a renowned real estate mogul, set an early goal of building a successful real estate agency. With a focus on scaling her business and maintaining top-tier client service, she turned a
$1,000 loan into a multimillion-dollar empire.

2. **Defining Your "Why"**

> **Identify personal motivations for investing**
  (e.g., financial freedom, early retirement, creating a legacy).
> **Your "why" influences your strategy and risk tolerance.**

3. **Short-Term vs. Long-Term Goals**

> **Short-Term Goals:**
  - Acquiring your first property.
  - Learning the basics of market analysis and financing.
  - Establishing a professional network.

> **Long-Term Goals:**
  - Building a portfolio with steady cash flow.
  - Achieving financial independence through passive income.
  - Scaling operations or diversifying investments.

4. **SMART Goals Framework**

> **Breaking down Specific, Measurable, Achievable, Relevant, and Time-Bound goals for real estate in- vesting.**
> **Examples:**

  - "Purchase my first investment property within six months with a budget of $200,000."

  - "Achieve a 10% ROI on rental properties within the first year."

5. **Aligning Goals with Investment Strategies**

> **Choosing strategies that suit your goals:**
  - Fix-and-flip for immediate returns.
  - Buy-and-hold for long-term growth.
  - Short-term rentals for cash flow.

6. **Assessing Your Resources and Constraints**

> **Evaluate your current financial situation and personal risk tolerance.**

> **Set realistic goals based on time, money, and experience.**

7. Revisiting and Adjusting Goals Over Time

> Be flexible as markets and personal circumstances change.

> Create a system to regularly review and update goals.

8. Action Steps to Get Started

> Write down your "why" and set at least three SMART goals for the next 12 months.

> Research one market that aligns with your investment goals.

> Share your goals with a mentor or accountability partner to stay on track.

Setting Clear Goals

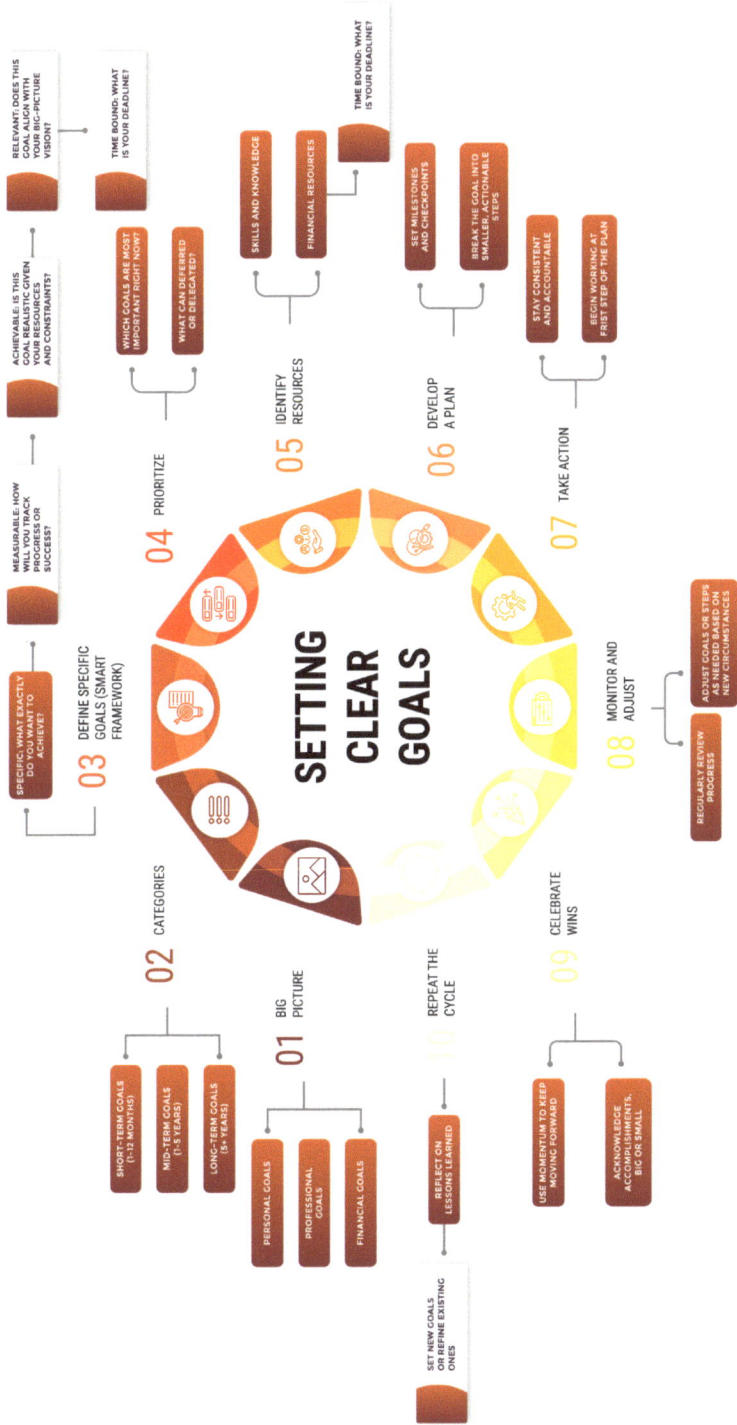

SETTING CLEAR GOALS

01 BIG PICTURE
- PERSONAL GOALS
- PROFESSIONAL GOALS
- FINANCIAL GOALS

02 CATEGORIES
- SHORT-TERM GOALS (1-12 MONTHS)
- MID-TERM GOALS (1-5 YEARS)
- LONG-TERM GOALS (5+ YEARS)

03 DEFINE SPECIFIC GOALS (SMART FRAMEWORK)
- SPECIFIC: WHAT EXACTLY DO YOU WANT TO ACHIEVE?
- MEASURABLE: HOW WILL YOU TRACK PROGRESS OR SUCCESS?
- ACHIEVABLE: IS THIS GOAL REALISTIC GIVEN YOUR RESOURCES AND CONSTRAINTS?
- RELEVANT: DOES THIS GOAL ALIGN WITH YOUR BIG-PICTURE VISION?
- TIME BOUND: WHAT IS YOUR DEADLINE?

04 PRIORITIZE
- WHICH GOALS ARE MOST IMPORTANT RIGHT NOW?
- WHAT CAN DEFERRED OR DELEGATED?

05 IDENTIFY RESOURCES
- SKILLS AND KNOWLEDGE
- FINANCIAL RESOURCES

06 DEVELOP A PLAN
- SET MILESTONES AND CHECKPOINTS
- BREAK THE GOAL INTO SMALLER, ACTIONABLE STEPS

07 TAKE ACTION
- STAY CONSISTENT AND ACCOUNTABLE
- BEGIN WORKING AT FRIST STEP OF THE PLAN

08 MONITOR AND ADJUST
- REGULARLY REVIEW PROGRESS
- ADJUST GOALS OR STEPS AS NEEDED BASED ON NEW CIRCUMSTANCES

09 CELEBRATE WINS
- USE MOMENTUM TO KEEP MOVING FORWARD
- ACKNOWLEDGE ACCOMPLISHMENTS, BIG OR SMALL

10 REPEAT THE CYCLE
- REFLECT ON LESSONS LEARNED
- SET NEW GOALS OR REFINE EXISTING ONES

CHAPTER 3

The Power of a Positive Mindset

Real estate investing is more than numbers, deals, and properties.

The way you think and approach challenges plays a pivotal role in your journey as an investor. A positive mindset doesn't just help you overcome obstacles-it positions you to recognize opportunities, build strong relationships, and stay focused on your goals, even in uncertain times.

Why Mindset Matters

Success in Real Estate investing requires more than technical skills. It demands resilience, creativity, and the ability to adapt to ever-changing circumstances. Market fluctuations, financing hurdles, and unforeseen challenges can shake even the most experienced investor. What separates those who thrive from those who falter is their mindset. With a positive outlook, you're more likely to approach problems as opportunities for growth rather than insurmountable barriers.

Developing a Growth Mindset

A growth mindset is the belief that your abilities and intelligence can be developed through effort and learning. In Real Estate, this translates to:

> **Embrace Failure as a Learning Opportunity:** Every setback, whether it's a deal that falls through or a miscalculated renovation budget, is a chance to gain valuable insights.

> **Seek Continuous Improvement:** Successful investors constantly educate themselves- reading books, attending seminars, networking, and staying updated on market trends.

> **Stay Open to New Strategies:** Flexibility is key. Markets change, and so do investment strategies. A growth mindset ensures you're willing to adapt when necessary.

Overcoming Negative Thinking

Even the most optimistic investors face moments of doubt. The key is not to let those thoughts dictate your actions. Here are some strategies to overcome negativity:

1. **Reframe Challenges:** Instead of seeing a problem as a roadblock, view it as a puzzle to solve.

2. **Practice Gratitude:** Focus on what's going well in your business. This perspective shift can boost your mood and motivation.

2. **Surround Yourself with Positivity:** Your network matters. Connect with people who inspire and encourage you rather than those who dwell on negativity.

The Ripple Effect of Positivity

A positive mindset doesn't just benefit you- it impacts everyone around you. Your optimism and resilience can inspire your team, build trust with clients, and strengthen your reputation in the industry. Confidence and positivity pull people in. How you treat others shapes your reputation and opens doors to the kind of opportunities and partners you want.

Practical Exercises to Build a Positive Mindset

1. **Daily Affirmations:** Rewire your mindset each morning. Statements like "I am more than capable of achieving my goals" or "Obstacles are just disguised invitations to grow" can help set the tone for your day.

2. **More than Visualization:** Picture your success. Whether it's closing a major deal, acquiring your dream property, or achieving financial independence. Visualizing your success is powerful- but the real work lies in how you feel during the visualization. Start by tapping into the excitement and gratitude you would feel if your goals were already achieved. This is just the beginning. There's a wealth of teachings on this topic, and you might want to start with the e-book included in your Free Bonus Action Plan. It's a great first step toward understanding these principles and putting them into practice.

Essential Teachings on Visualization, Belief & Emotional Alignment

1. The Law of Success in 16 Lessons by Napoleon Hill (e-book in your Free Bonus Action Plan)

   A comprehensive guide to achieving success through desire, faith, initiative, and self-discipline, laying the foundation for modern personal development.

2. Think and Grow Rich by Napoleon Hill

   Focuses on the power of the mind to create wealth and success, with visualization, belief, and autosuggestion as key tools.

3. The Bible

   Scripture is rich with teachings on faith, vision, and the power of belief:
   - "As a man thinketh in his heart, so is he." - Proverbs 23:7
   - "Write the vision and make it plain..." - Habakkuk 2:2
   - "Faith is the substance of things hoped for, the evidence of things not seen." - Hebrews 11:1

   These verses reinforce that internal belief precedes external manifestation.

4. Your Wish is Your Command by Kevin Trudeau

   An audio/book teaching elite level strategies on thoughts, beliefs, and emotions to create wealth, freedom, and success in every area of your life.

5. As a Man Thinketh by James Allen

   A foundational work illustrating how thought and character determine destiny-your inner world creates your outer world.

6. The Strangest Secret by Earl Nightingale

   A short but powerful audio/book that states: "You become what you think about." Focused thought, paired with faith and action, leads to success.

7. Psycho-Cybernetics by Dr. Maxwell Maltz

   Introduces the concept of the "theater of the mind" and how visualization rewires self-image, which in turn reshapes results.

8. You Were Born Rich by Bob Proctor
   Builds on Hill's teachings and shows how to apply visualization and emotion to unlock your God-given potential for abundance.

9. The Game of Life and How to Play It by Florence Scovel Shinn
   A spiritually grounded guide to manifesting through words, thoughts, and belief, highlighting faith in divine timing and guidance.

Quantum physics reveals that, at the deepest level, reality is made of energy and frequency. Within this framework, our thoughts and emotions generate energetic patterns – vibrations that shape how we experience and influence the world around us. This supports the idea that cultivating a positive mindset not only shifts our perception but also attracts the opportunities and success we seek. This concept aligns with the principle of resonance-where like attracts like-and our internal frequencies harmonize with the external environment, amplifying our potential for growth, prosperity, and well-being.

By consciously turning our mindset to a higher frequency, such as embodying qualities like compassion, gratitude, and faith, we align ourselves with a divine frequency that supports growth and success. When we approach challenges with a mindset of love, compassion, and positivity, we create an energetic resonance that attracts similar frequencies-whether it's support from others,

opportunities for personal growth, or the ability to navigate difficulties with grace. This higher frequency not only elevates our well-being but also influences those around us, creating a ripple effect of positivity, compassion, and connection.

3. **Mindfulness and Reflection:** Take time to reflect on your work. Praying, meditating, or journaling can help you process your experiences and stay grounded.

Building Confidence Through Action

Confidence comes from doing. The more you immerse yourself in the world of Real Estate by analyzing deals, meeting professionals, and taking calculated risks, the more self-assured you'll become. Start small, celebrate your wins, and use each success as a stepping stone to greater achievements.

A positive mindset empowers you to navigate challenges, seize opportunities, and inspire others along the way. By cultivating optimism, resilience, and a growth-oriented approach, you're not just building a portfolio, you're creating a legacy.

The most valuable asset in your Real Estate business isn't a property or a deal;
it's your mindset!

The Power Of A Positive Mindset
A growth mindset attribute

> Look for lessons in every stumble

> See every failure as a stepping stone to growth

> Stay Open to New Strategies

> Reframe Challenges

> Practice Gratitude

> Surround Yourself with Positivity

CHAPTER 4

Understanding Your Financials

To start investing, it's crucial to have a clear picture of your current financial situation and plan how you'll finance your investments. It's not just about knowing your credit score or available funds- it's about having a clear picture of your overall financial health and aligning it with your investment goals. This includes tracking income, expenses, and savings, as well as planning for potential risks.

Analyze Your Financial Position

Before diving into real estate investing, it's crucial to take a detailed look at your current financial position. Start by evaluating your savings to determine how much capital you can allocate to your first investment. Review your credit score, as this will affect the financing options and interest rates available to you. Consider your existing debts, such as student loans, car payments, or credit card balances, and assess how they impact your ability to take on additional obligations. Lastly, identify your risk tolerance-how comfortable are you with financial risks, and how much are you willing to lose in a worst-case scenario? This analysis provides a clear foundation for planning your investments strategically and responsibly.

Determine Your Investment Budget

Once you've assessed your financial position, set a realistic investment budget. This includes not only the amount you're willing to spend on acquiring a property but also additional costs such as closing costs, property inspections, insurance, and renovations. It's equally important to establish a contingency fund, aim to have at least 3-6 months of expenses set aside for unexpected repairs, vacancies, or economic downturns.

Avoid allocating all your savings to a single property; keeping reserves ensures you can weather financial challenges without jeopardizing your overall stability.

Planning your budget is a cornerstone of long-term success in real estate investing.

Explore Financing Options

Understanding your financing options is a critical step in making informed investment decisions.

> Traditional mortgages are popular for their lower interest rates and longer terms but may require a substantial down payment.

> Hard money loans offer quicker approval processes and are ideal for short-term projects like flips but come with higher interest rates.

> Private loans, often from individuals or small groups, provide flexible terms that can be tailored to your needs, making them an attractive option for unconventional deals.

> Partnerships are another avenue-working with others can help you pool resources and reduce individual risk.

Each option has its advantages and challenges, so research and consult with financial advisors or mortgage brokers to choose the one that aligns with your investment strategy. *(See Chapter 7.)*

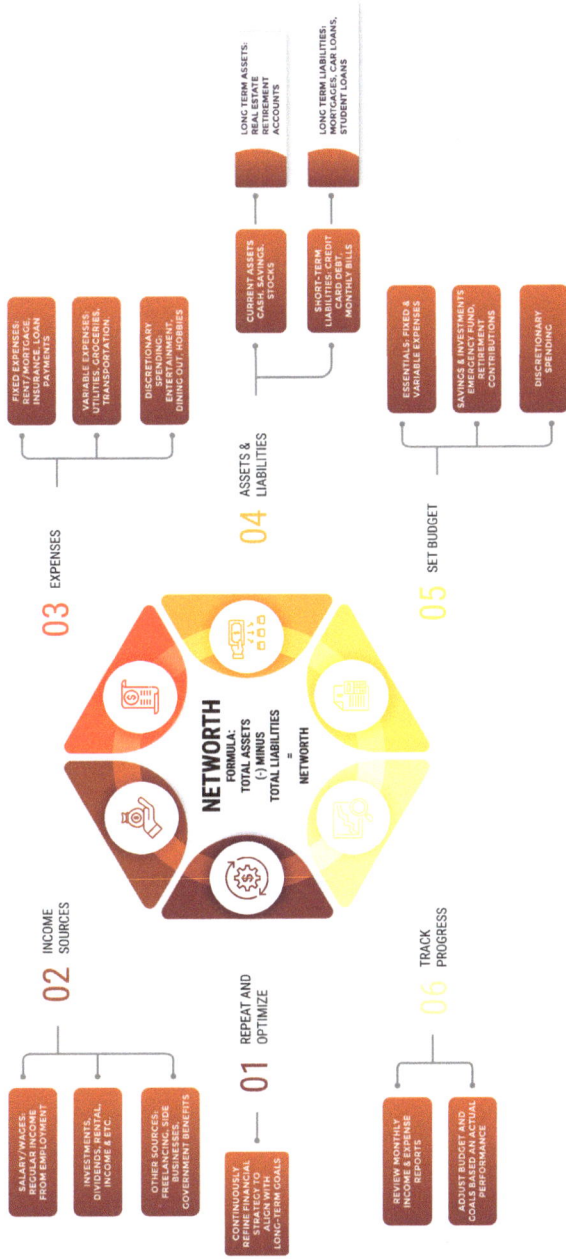

Understanding Your Financials

NETWORTH

FORMULA:
TOTAL ASSETS
(-) MINUS
TOTAL LIABILITIES
=
NETWORTH

01 REPEAT AND OPTIMIZE

- CONTINUOUSLY REFINE FINANCIAL STRATEGY TO ALIGN WITH LONG-TERM GOALS

02 INCOME SOURCES

- SALARY/WAGES: REGULAR INCOME FROM EMPLOYMENT
- INVESTMENTS: DIVIDENDS, RENTAL INCOME & ETC.
- OTHER SOURCES: FREELANCING, SIDE BUSINESSES, GOVERNMENT BENEFITS

03 EXPENSES

- FIXED EXPENSES: RENT/MORTGAGE, INSURANCE, LOAN PAYMENTS
- VARIABLE EXPENSES: UTILITIES, GROCERIES, TRANSPORTATION
- DISCRETIONARY SPENDING: ENTERTAINMENT, DINING OUT, HOBBIES

04 ASSETS & LIABILITIES

- CURRENT ASSETS: CASH, SAVINGS, STOCKS
- SHORT-TERM LIABILITIES: CREDIT CARD DEBT, MONTHLY BILLS
- LONG TERM ASSETS: REAL ESTATE, RETIREMENT ACCOUNTS
- LONG TERM LIABILITIES: MORTGAGES, CAR LOANS, STUDENT LOANS

05 SET BUDGET

- ESSENTIALS: FIXED & VARIABLE EXPENSES
- SAVINGS & INVESTMENTS: EMERGENCY FUND, RETIREMENT CONTRIBUTIONS
- DISCRETIONARY SPENDING

06 TRACK PROGRESS

- REVIEW MONTHLY INCOME & EXPENSE REPORTS
- ADJUST BUDGET AND GOALS BASED ON ACTUAL PERFORMANCE

21

CHAPTER 5
Building a Team

Real estate investing can be complex, so building a strong team will help you navigate it smoothly.

Key Team Members to Consider:

> **Real Estate Agent:** To help find and negotiate deals. Focus on agents experienced in investment properties who can spot good deals and understand cash flow. Ask for referrals or review testimonials to gauge their performance.

> **Mortgage Broker:** To secure the best financing options. A mortgage broker acts as an intermediary between you and lenders, helping you find the best financing options. They have access to multiple-loan products, often beyond what traditional banks offer, which can be especially valuable for investors.

> **Real Estate Appraiser:** For accurate measurements and value. A Real Estate Appraiser provides an objective valuation of a property, which is crucial for making informed investment decisions. Independent Real Estate Appraisers can help you avoid overpaying for a property and understand its true market value. They also offer accurate property measurements and details on comparable sales in the area.

> **Property Manager:** To handle tenant and maintenance issues. If you plan to outsource management, select someone with local market knowledge. Ensure they understand your goals, such as prioritizing tenant retention or property appreciation.

> **Contractors and Maintenance Professionals:** For repairs, renovations, and upgrades. Establish relationships with reliable contractors for renovations and maintenance work. Get quotes from multiple sources and review previous projects.

> **Accountant:** Work with professionals skilledin real estate tax strategies. They can help you maximize deductions and structure finances efficiently.

- **Attorney:** For legal and financial advice. Retain a lawyer familiar with real estate contracts, zoning laws, and tenant regulations. This will protect you from legal pitfalls as you grow your portfolio.
- **Mentors or Coaches:** Partner with experienced investors who can guide you in decision-making. They can provide real-world advice that accelerates your learning curve.

How to Find Team Members

1. **Networking Events**
   - Attend local meetups, conferences, or investment clubs (REIA's) to meet potential team members.
   - Look for professionals with a collaborative attitude and proven experience.
2. **Referrals**
   - Leverage your current network for recommendations.
   - Ask other investors, friends, or colleagues for trusted contacts.
3. **Online Platforms**
   - Use tools like LinkedIn, BiggerPockets, or local Facebook groups to connect with Real Estate professionals.
4. **Trial Periods**
   - Start with smaller tasks, look for Turnkey Investments Near You (TINY) or smaller projects to assess a potential team member's skills and reliability. In real estate, a turnkey property is a property that is ready to be used or rented out (often furnished) without any major work or repairs.

Building Your Team

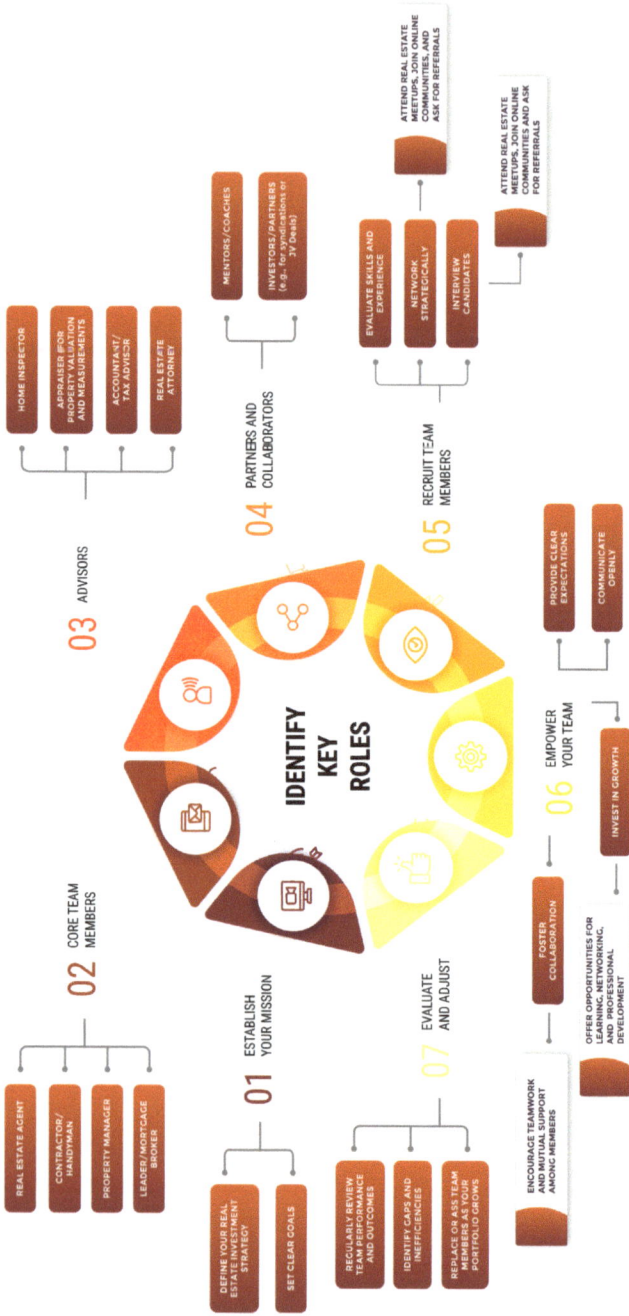

IDENTIFY KEY ROLES

01 ESTABLISH YOUR MISSION
- DEFINE YOUR REAL ESTATE INVESTMENT STRATEGY
- SET CLEAR GOALS

02 CORE TEAM MEMBERS
- REAL ESTATE AGENT
- CONTRACTOR/HANDYMAN
- PROPERTY MANAGER
- LENDER/MORTGAGE BROKER

03 ADVISORS
- HOME INSPECTOR
- APPRAISER (FOR PROPERTY VALUATION AND MEASUREMENTS)
- ACCOUNTANT/TAX ADVISOR
- REAL ESTATE ATTORNEY

04 PARTNERS AND COLLABORATORS
- MENTORS/COACHES
- INVESTORS/PARTNERS (e.g., for syndications or JV Deals)

05 RECRUIT TEAM MEMBERS
- EVALUATE SKILLS AND EXPERIENCE
- NETWORK STRATEGICALLY
- INTERVIEW CANDIDATES
- ATTEND REAL ESTATE MEETUPS, JOIN ONLINE COMMUNITIES, AND ASK FOR REFERRALS
- ATTEND REAL ESTATE MEETUPS, JOIN ONLINE COMMUNITIES AND ASK FOR REFERRALS

06 EMPOWER YOUR TEAM
- PROVIDE CLEAR EXPECTATIONS
- COMMUNICATE OPENLY
- INVEST IN GROWTH
- FOSTER COLLABORATION
- OFFER OPPORTUNITIES FOR LEARNING, NETWORKING, AND PROFESSIONAL DEVELOPMENT
- ENCOURAGE TEAMWORK AND MUTUAL SUPPORT AMONG MEMBERS

07 EVALUATE AND ADJUST
- REGULARLY REVIEW TEAM PERFORMANCE AND OUTCOMES
- IDENTIFY GAPS AND INEFFICIENCIES
- REPLACE OR ADD TEAM MEMBERS AS YOUR PORTFOLIO GROWS

CHAPTER 6

Identifying Investment Strategies

There are various strategies you can use depending on your goals, risk tolerance, and finances.

Common Real Estate Investment Strategies:

1. **Buy and Hold:** Purchase properties, rent them out, and hold them for long-term appreciation.

2. **Fix and Flip:** Purchase properties at a discount, renovate, and sell for profit.

3. **Wholesaling:** Contract a property with the intent to sell the contract to another investor.

4. **House Hacking:** Purchase a multi-unit property, live in one unit, and rent the others to cover your mortgage.

5. **Short-Term Rentals:** Renting out properties on a short-term basis (e.g., Airbnb or vacation rentals).

6. **Syndication** - Pooling resources from multiple investors to acquire larger properties, usually involves a syndicator or sponsor managing the deal while investors contribute capital.

7. **BRRRR Method** - Buy, Rehab, Rent, Refinance, Repeat: Build a portfolio by recycling capital.

   > **Buy:** Purchase undervalued or distressed properties.

   > **Rehab:** Renovate to increase property value and rental appeal.

   > **Rent:** Lease the property to generate steady cash flow.

   > **Refinance:** Refinance the property to pull out equity for future investments.

   > **Repeat:** Use the extracted funds to acquire additional properties.

Identifying Investment Strategies

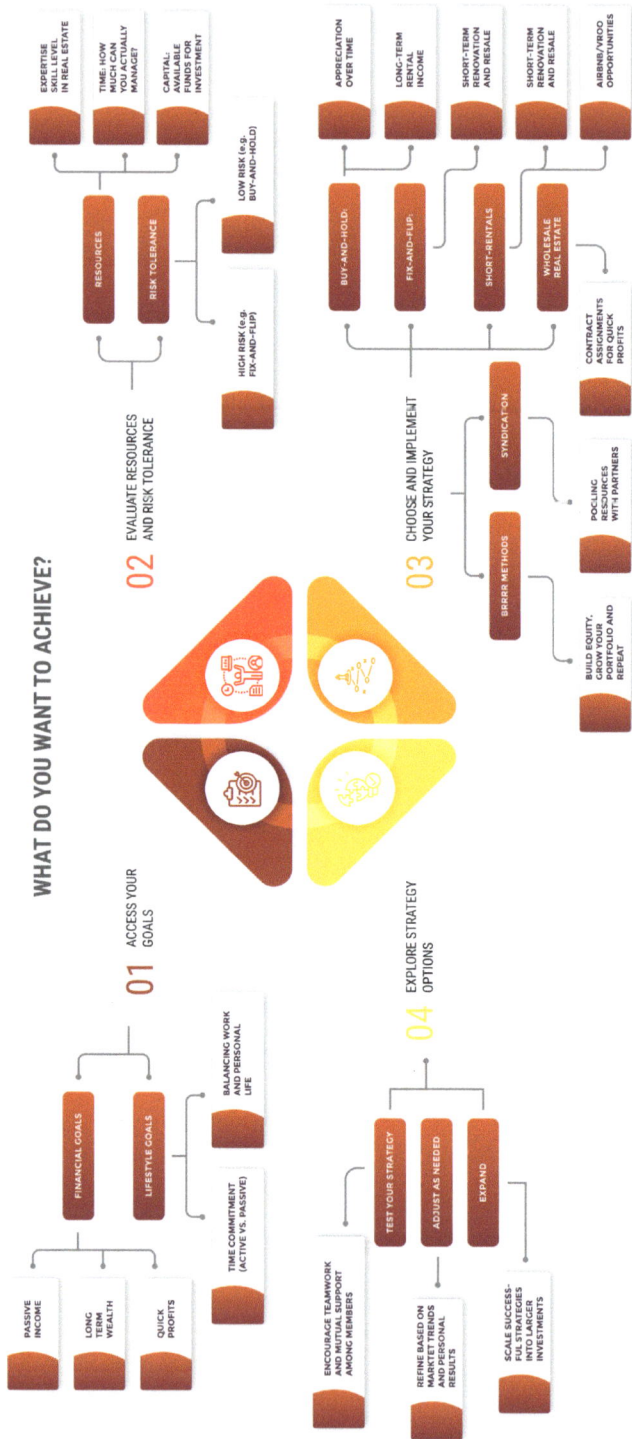

WHAT DO YOU WANT TO ACHIEVE?

01 ACCESS YOUR GOALS

- FINANCIAL GOALS
  - PASSIVE INCOME
  - LONG TERM WEALTH
  - QUICK PROFITS
- LIFESTYLE GOALS
  - TIME COMMITMENT (ACTIVE VS. PASSIVE)
  - BALANCING WORK AND PERSONAL LIFE

02 EVALUATE RESOURCES AND RISK TOLERANCE

- RESOURCES
  - EXPERTISE: SKILL LEVEL IN REAL ESTATE
  - TIME: HOW MUCH CAN YOU ACTUALLY MANAGE?
  - CAPITAL: AVAILABLE FUNDS FOR INVESTMENT
- RISK TOLERANCE
  - LOW RISK (e.g. BUY-AND-HOLD)
  - HIGH RISK (e.g. FIX-AND-FLIP)

03 CHOOSE AND IMPLEMENT YOUR STRATEGY

- BUY-AND-HOLD
  - APPRECIATION OVER TIME
  - LONG-TERM RENTAL INCOME
- FIX-AND-FLIP
  - SHORT-TERM RENOVATION AND RESALE
  - SHORT-TERM RENOVATION AND RESALE
- SHORT-RENTALS
  - AIRBNB/VRBO OPPORTUNITIES
- WHOLESALE REAL ESTATE
  - CONTRACT ASSIGNMENTS FOR QUICK PROFITS
- SYNDICATION
  - POOLING RESOURCES WITH PARTNERS
- BRRRR METHODS
  - BUILD EQUITY, GROW YOUR PORTFOLIO AND REPEAT

04 EXPLORE STRATEGY OPTIONS

- TEST YOUR STRATEGY
  - ENCOURAGE TEAMWORK AND MUTUAL SUPPORT AMONG MEMBERS
- ADJUST AS NEEDED
  - REFINE BASED ON MARKET TRENDS AND PERSONAL RESULTS
- EXPAND
  - SCALE SUCCESSFUL STRATEGIES INTO LARGER INVESTMENTS

26

CHAPTER 7

Market Research and Finding Deals

Choosing the right market and finding the right property are essential. Here's what you need to focus on:

1. Market Analysis: Identify locations with high demand, stable or growing population, and positive economic indicators

Tools for Market Analysis:

> **Comparative Market Analysis (CMA) Tools**: These are used to evaluate similar properties (comps) in the area to estimate a property's market value. Popular tools include:

- **Zillow:** Provides property estimates and sale prices for homes in each area. **Always hire a Real Estate Appraiser for accurate property values**.
- Redfin: Offers real-time data and detailed property history.
- **Realtor.com:** Includes information about sales, neighborhood insights, and current listings.
- **MLS** (Multiple Listing Service): Accessed through real estate agents, offering the most accurate and up-to-date market data.

> **Real Estate Investment Software:** These tools help investors analyze potential investments and assess cash flow, ROI, and market trends.

- **PropStream:** Helps analyze properties for flips, rentals, or wholesale deals, providing real-time data.
- **Mashvisor:** Offers data on rental properties and insights for both short-term and long-term investments.
- **CoStar:** A powerful tool for analyzing commercial properties and understanding broader market trends.

> **Market Research Websites:** Some websites provide free market trend insights and local economic data.

- **Trulia:** Offers neighborhood data including crime rates, school ratings, and nearby amenities.
- **Local Government Websites:** Often provide economic reports, demographic data, and future development plans.

> **Geographic Information Systems (GIS):** These tools help in mapping out data related to specific locations, showing trends, zoning, and land use. Examples include **ESRI ArcGIS and MapInfo.**

> **Role of Real Estate Agents in Market Analysis**

- **Local Market Knowledge:** Realtors with strong local knowledge can provide valuable insights on current trends, neighborhood shifts, and emerging investment opportunities.
- **Comparative Market Analysis (CMA):** Realtors can run detailed CMAs, offering guidance on how similar properties are performing and helping investors price properties effectively.
- **Neighborhood Expertise:** Experienced realtors often have up-to-date information about school districts, crime rates, and community developments that could influence market trends.
- **Negotiation Expertise:** A realtor can help negotiate the best price for a property based on market trends and comparable sales.

Property Analysis: Look for properties in areas with high rent demand and good appreciation potential.

Tools for Market Analysis:

> **Cash Flow:** Income after expenses.
> **Cap Rate:** Annual return on investment.
> **Cash-on-Cash Return:** ROI based on the amount of cash invested.

Cost Estimation Tools:

> **Cost Estimator:** Provides detailed repair and renovation cost analysis for properties.

> **Build Zoom:** Helps analyze contractor bids and renovation costs in your area.

> **REI Hub:** Combines property financial data and analysis, showing cash flow and ROI potential.

> **Finding Deals:** Use real estate websites, foreclosure listings, auctions, networking, and driving neighborhoods to find off-market deals.

- **Helping Homeowners in Difficult Situations** As a real estate investor, one of the most impactful roles you can take on is to offer a helping hand to homeowners in distress. When you come across someone facing foreclosure, divorce, financial hardship, or any other challenging life situation, you have the opportunity to make a positive difference by providing a solution that benefits both parties.

- **Pre-Foreclosure and Beyond** Homeowners in pre-foreclosure are often overwhelmed with the threat of losing their property, but many don't know that they may have options outside of a traditional foreclosure.

- As an investor, your job is to understand their situation and offer viable alternatives, whether that's buying their property outright or working with them to find a creative solution, like lease options or seller financing.

  It is important to approach them with empathy and understanding, ensuring they know you're here to help, not just to profit.

- **Providing Value in Every Deal** Your ultimate goal as an investor should not be just to acquire properties at discounted rates, but to genuinely solve problems for homeowners. Whether they need fast cash or a way out of a burdensome mortgage, helping them navigate their options can lead to long-term relationships and a positive reputation. When you offer homeowners peace of mind and a fair, transparent process, you're helping to restore stability in their lives while also building trust within your network.

By prioritizing the well-being of homeowners and focusing on creating win-win solutions, you enhance your own success as an investor and contribute positively to the community.

> **Real Estate Websites:**

- **MLS (Multiple Listing Service):** Accessible through realtors, the MLS is a comprehensive database of properties listed for sale. It includes details like price history, market trends, and property features.
- **Zillow and Realtor.com:** Great for identifying active listings and understanding market trends in your area.
- **LoopNet:** A valuable resource for commercial real estate deals, including multifamily, office, and retail properties.
- **Auction.com:** Specializes in foreclosed properties and online auctions.
- **BiggerPockets Marketplace:** A platform for investors to find off-market deals and network with other investors.

2. **Foreclosure Listings**

> **County Websites:** Many local governments post foreclosure and tax lien listings on their official websites.

> **Foreclosure-Specific Platforms:**

- **Foreclosure.com:** Offers nationwide listings of foreclosures, pre-foreclosures, and bank-owned properties (REOs).
- **Hubzu:** Focuses on online foreclosure auctions, often with properties priced below market value.

> **Banks and Lenders:** Many banks have departments or websites dedicated to listing REO properties.

3. **Real Estate Auctions**

> **In-Person Auctions:** Check local courthouse schedules for property auctions in your area. These often feature foreclosed properties sold to the highest bidder.

- **Online Auctions:**
  - **Auction.com:** Offers a wide range of properties, including residential, commercial, and land.
  - **Hubzu:** Allows investors to bid online, often providing detailed property information.
  - **Xome:** A user-friendly auction site with live and online options.
- **Tips for Auctions:**
  - Research property conditions beforehand, as most auctions are sold "as-is."
  - Be prepared to act quickly, as auctions often require immediate payment.

4. **Networking**
  - **Real Estate Investor Associations (REIAs):** Join local or online groups to connect with wholesalers, real estate agents, and other investors.
  - **Wholesalers:** Build relationships with wholesalers who specialize in finding discounted properties for investors.
  - **Real Estate Agents:** Partner with agents who focus on investment properties or have connections to off-market deals.
  - **Social media:** Use platforms like Facebook Groups, LinkedIn, and Instagram to connect with sellers and investors who might share leads.

5. **Driving for Dollars**
  - **Identifying Potential Properties:** Drive through neighborhoods and look for signs of distressed properties, such as overgrown lawns, peeling paint, or boarded windows.
  - **Technology to Enhance Driving for Dollars:**
    - **DealMachine:** A mobile app that allows you to instantly capture property information, track leads, and even send direct mail to property owners.
    - **LandGlide:** Provides parcel data to quickly identify property owners and details.

> **Direct Outreach:** Once you identify a property, contact the owner via phone, email, or mail to express interest in purchasing.

6. Off-Market Deal Platforms

> **CREXi:** Focuses on commercial real estate and off-market opportunities.

> **Pocket Listings:** Work with agents who can share properties not yet listed publicly.

> **Local Networking Events:** Attend real estate meetups (RFIA's), auctions, or community gatherings to hear about properties before they hit the market.

7. Public Recordsand Data Sources

> **Tax Lien Records:** Many counties post tax-delinquent properties, which can be opportunities for investors.

> **Probate Listings:** Look for properties in probate court that may be sold below market value.

> **Vacancy Lists:** Data providers like Vacant House Data Feed offer lists of vacant properties, which are prime candidates for off-market deals.

Finding Deals

MARKET RESEARCH

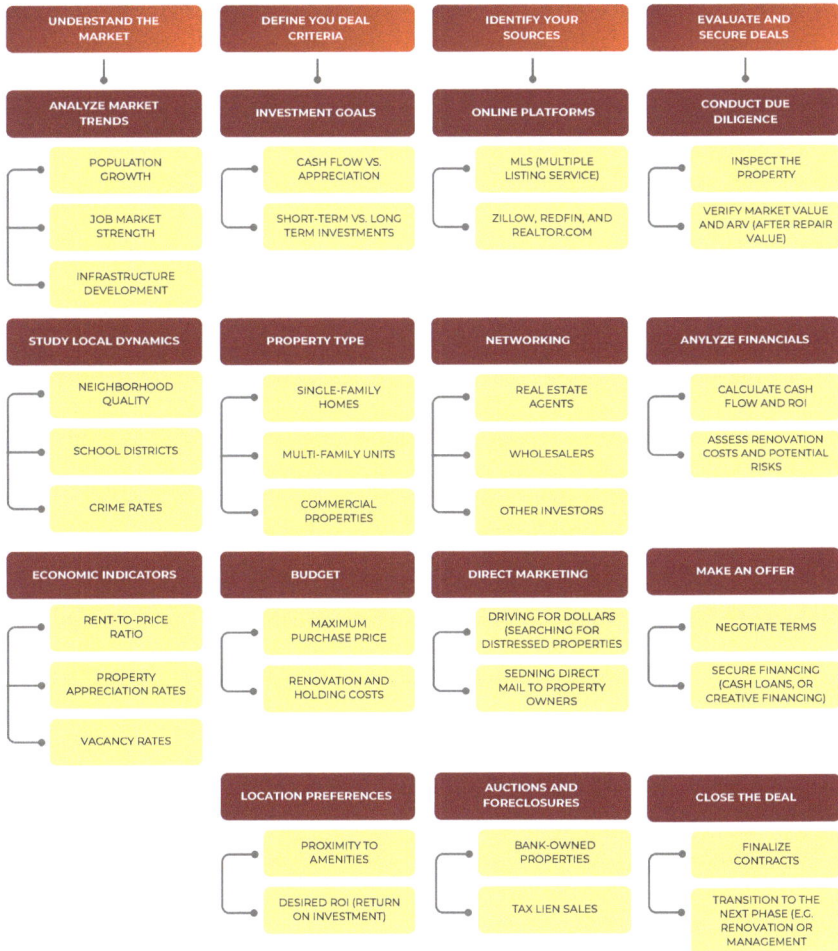

UNDERSTAND THE MARKET	DEFINE YOU DEAL CRITERIA	IDENTIFY YOUR SOURCES	EVALUATE AND SECURE DEALS

ANALYZE MARKET TRENDS
- POPULATION GROWTH
- JOB MARKET STRENGTH
- INFRASTRUCTURE DEVELOPMENT

INVESTMENT GOALS
- CASH FLOW VS. APPRECIATION
- SHORT-TERM VS. LONG TERM INVESTMENTS

ONLINE PLATFORMS
- MLS (MULTIPLE LISTING SERVICE)
- ZILLOW, REDFIN, AND REALTOR.COM

CONDUCT DUE DILIGENCE
- INSPECT THE PROPERTY
- VERIFY MARKET VALUE AND ARV (AFTER REPAIR VALUE)

STUDY LOCAL DYNAMICS
- NEIGHBORHOOD QUALITY
- SCHOOL DISTRICTS
- CRIME RATES

PROPERTY TYPE
- SINGLE-FAMILY HOMES
- MULTI-FAMILY UNITS
- COMMERCIAL PROPERTIES

NETWORKING
- REAL ESTATE AGENTS
- WHOLESALERS
- OTHER INVESTORS

ANYLYZE FINANCIALS
- CALCULATE CASH FLOW AND ROI
- ASSESS RENOVATION COSTS AND POTENTIAL RISKS

ECONOMIC INDICATORS
- RENT-TO-PRICE RATIO
- PROPERTY APPRECIATION RATES
- VACANCY RATES

BUDGET
- MAXIMUM PURCHASE PRICE
- RENOVATION AND HOLDING COSTS

DIRECT MARKETING
- DRIVING FOR DOLLARS (SEARCHING FOR DISTRESSED PROPERTIES
- SEDNING DIRECT MAIL TO PROPERTY OWNERS

MAKE AN OFFER
- NEGOTIATE TERMS
- SECURE FINANCING (CASH LOANS, OR CREATIVE FINANCING)

LOCATION PREFERENCES
- PROXIMITY TO AMENITIES
- DESIRED ROI (RETURN ON INVESTMENT)

AUCTIONS AND FORECLOSURES
- BANK-OWNED PROPERTIES
- TAX LIEN SALES

CLOSE THE DEAL
- FINALIZE CONTRACTS
- TRANSITION TO THE NEXT PHASE (E.G. RENOVATION OR MANAGEMENT

Financing Your Deal

Decide on a financing strategy based on your chosen investment and financial capacity.

1. Traditional Financing Options

> **Mortgages:**
  - Conventional loans.
  - Government-backed loans (FHA, VA) for specific buyer profiles.

> **Home Equity Line of Credit or HELOCs:**
  - Leveraging existing property equity to fund new investments.

2. Creative Financing Strategies

> **Owner Financing:**
  - Negotiate directly with the seller, no bank needed.

> **Lease Options:**
  - "Rent-to-own" to control properties without immediate ownership.

3. Partnering with Others

> **Joint Ventures:**
  - Pooling resources and sharing responsibilities with other investors.

Syndication:
  - Group investments for larger deals *(see Chapter 5)*.

4. Alternative Funding Sources

> **Hard Money Loans:**
  - Short-term, high-interest loans for quick property flips.

> **Private Lenders:**
  - Securing funds from individuals for flexible terms.

> **Crowdfunding:**
  - Platforms that connect investors for real estate projects.

5. **Leveraging the BRRRR Strategy for Financing**

> How refinancing under the BRRRR method provides continual funding.
> Scaling your portfolio without repeatedly saving for down payments.

6. **Grants and Incentives**

> Exploring local and federal programs for real estate investors.
> Tax credits for specific types of properties (e.g., historic or energy-efficient buildings).

7. **Building Relationships with Lenders**

> Build a strong credit score and financial history.
> Network with local banks, credit unions, and private lenders.
> Maintain open communication to secure favorable terms.

8. **Risk Management in Financing**

> Avoid over-leverage and manage debt responsibly.
> Maintain cash reserves for unforeseen expenses.
> Stress-testing your portfolio for market downturns.

FINANCING YOUR DEAL

WHAT DO YOU WANT TO ACHIEVE?

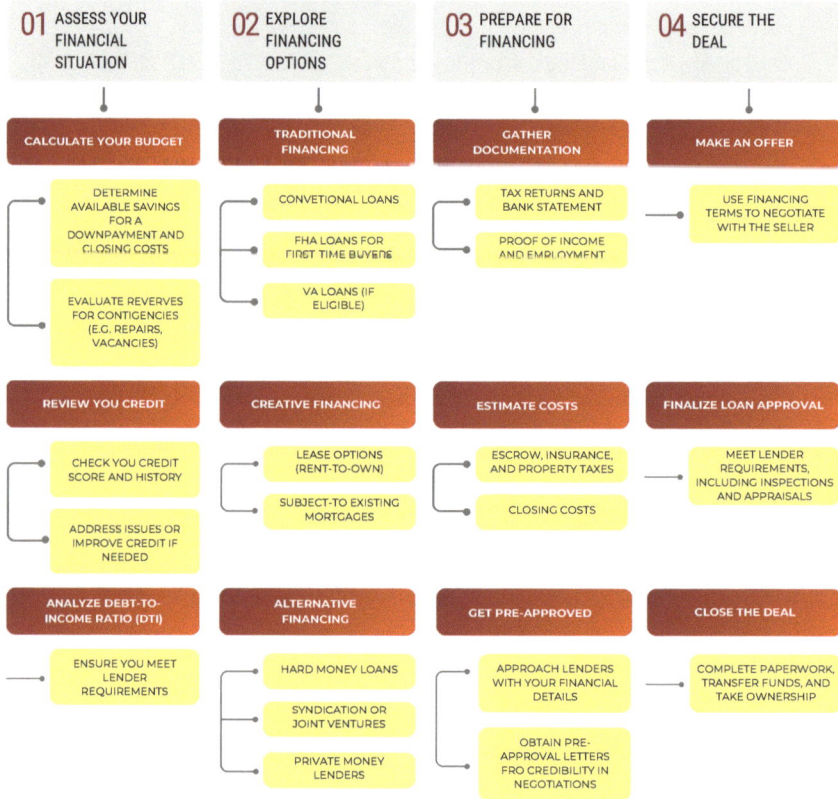

01 ASSESS YOUR FINANCIAL SITUATION

CALCULATE YOUR BUDGET

- DETERMINE AVAILABLE SAVINGS FOR A DOWNPAYMENT AND CLOSING COSTS
- EVALUATE REVERVES FOR CONTIGENCIES (E.G. REPAIRS, VACANCIES)

REVIEW YOU CREDIT

- CHECK YOU CREDIT SCORE AND HISTORY
- ADDRESS ISSUES OR IMPROVE CREDIT IF NEEDED

ANALYZE DEBT-TO-INCOME RATIO (DTI)

- ENSURE YOU MEET LENDER REQUIREMENTS

02 EXPLORE FINANCING OPTIONS

TRADITIONAL FINANCING

- CONVETIONAL LOANS
- FHA LOANS FOR FIRST TIME BUYERS
- VA LOANS (IF ELIGIBLE)

CREATIVE FINANCING

- LEASE OPTIONS (RENT-TO-OWN)
- SUBJECT-TO EXISTING MORTGAGES

ALTERNATIVE FINANCING

- HARD MONEY LOANS
- SYNDICATION OR JOINT VENTURES
- PRIVATE MONEY LENDERS

03 PREPARE FOR FINANCING

GATHER DOCUMENTATION

- TAX RETURNS AND BANK STATEMENT
- PROOF OF INCOME AND EMPLOYMENT

ESTIMATE COSTS

- ESCROW, INSURANCE, AND PROPERTY TAXES
- CLOSING COSTS

GET PRE-APPROVED

- APPROACH LENDERS WITH YOUR FINANCIAL DETAILS
- OBTAIN PRE-APPROVAL LETTERS FRO CREDIBILITY IN NEGOTIATIONS

04 SECURE THE DEAL

MAKE AN OFFER

- USE FINANCING TERMS TO NEGOTIATE WITH THE SELLER

FINALIZE LOAN APPROVAL

- MEET LENDER REQUIREMENTS, INCLUDING INSPECTIONS AND APPRAISALS

CLOSE THE DEAL

- COMPLETE PAPERWORK, TRANSFER FUNDS, AND TAKE OWNERSHIP

CHAPTER 9

Property Management

If you are investing in rental properties, effective management is key to generating consistent cash flow.

1. **The Role of Effective Property Management**

> Ensuring properties remain profitable and well-maintained.

> Building trust with tenants to minimize turnover.

> Protecting your investment throughproactive care.

2. **Self-Management vs. Hiring a Property Manager**

> **Self-Management:**
  - Benefits: Cost savings, direct tenant relationships.
  - Challenges: Time-intensive, requires hands-on involvement.

> **Professional Property Managers:**
  - Benefits: Experience, communication skills, operations already in place.
  - Challenges: Fees, requires managing the managers.

3. **Establishing Systems for Efficiency**

Tenant Screening

1. **Cozy (now part of Apartments.com):** A tool for tenant screening that provides credit reports, background checks, and income verification in one platform.

2. **MySmart Move by TransUnion:** Offers comprehensive tenant screening reports, including credit, eviction history, and criminal records.

Rent Collection

1. **Buildium:** Property management software that allows tenants to pay rent online and helps landlords track payments and manage late fees.

2. **PayRent:** A secure rent collection platform that enables online payments, auto-reminders, and late fee enforcement.

Maintenance Requests

1. **Property Meld:** A maintenance management system that facilitates communication between tenants, landlords, and maintenance staff, while tracking the progress of repair requests.

2. **AppFolio:** A property management tool with a maintenance request feature that allows tenants to submit requests online and helps property managers prioritize and resolve issues efficiently.

4. Legal Compliance in Property Management

> Adhering to local landlord-tenant laws.

> Understanding fair housing regulations and eviction processes.

> Maintaining accurate records for leases, payments, and inspections.

5. Tenant Relationships and Retention

> Building a rapport with tenants to encourage long- term leases.
> Handling disputes and complaints professionally.
> Creating incentives for renewals, such as minor upgrades or rent freezes.

6. Managing Multi-Unit Properties

> Unique challenges of apartment complexes and other multi-family properties.
> Hiring on-site managers or caretakers for larger complexes.
> Conduct regular inspections to ensure common areas are well-kept.

7. Tools and Technology for Property Management

> Property management software for tracking payments, leases, and maintenance.
> Apps and platforms for efficient tenant communication.
> Using analytics to monitor property performance and expenses.

8. Preparing for Unexpected Situations

> Handling emergencies like plumbing failures or natural disasters.
> Setting up an emergency fund for sudden expenses.
> Crafting contingency plans for economic down turns or tenant defaults.

PROPERTY MANAGEMENT

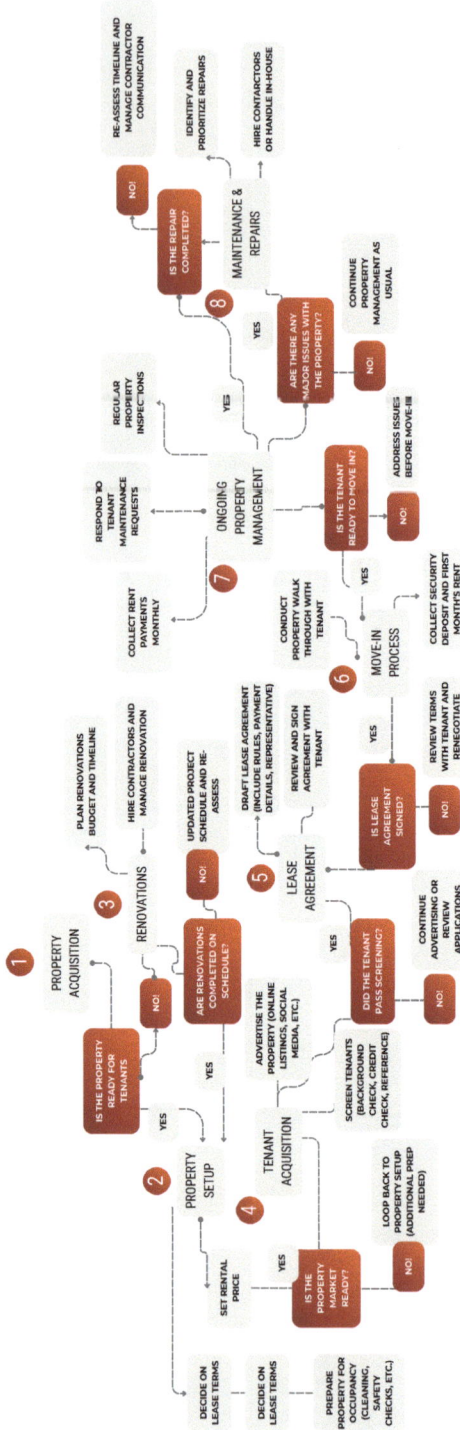

1. PROPERTY ACQUISITION
- IS THE PROPERTY READY FOR TENANTS?
  - NO! → RENOVATIONS (3)
    - PLAN RENOVATIONS BUDGET AND TIMELINE
    - HIRE CONTRACTORS AND MANAGE RENOVATION
    - ARE RENOVATIONS COMPLETED ON SCHEDULE?
      - NO! → UPDATED PROJECT SCHEDULE AND RE-ASSESS
      - YES
  - YES

2. PROPERTY SETUP
- SET RENTAL PRICE
- DECIDE ON LEASE TERMS
- DECIDE ON LEASE TERMS
- PREPARE PROPERTY FOR OCCUPANCY (CLEANING, SAFETY CHECKS, ETC.)
- IS THE PROPERTY MARKET READY?
  - NO! → LOOP BACK TO PROPERTY SETUP (ADDITIONAL PREP NEEDED)
  - YES

4. TENANT ACQUISITION
- ADVERTISE THE PROPERTY (ONLINE LISTINGS, SOCIAL MEDIA, ETC.)
- SCREEN TENANTS (BACKGROUND CHECK, CREDIT CHECK, REFERENCE)
- DID THE TENANT PASS SCREENING?
  - NO! → CONTINUE ADVERTISING OR REVIEW APPLICATIONS
  - YES

5. LEASE AGREEMENT
- DRAFT LEASE AGREEMENT (INCLUDE RULES, PAYMENT DETAILS, REPRESENTATIVE)
- REVIEW AND SIGN AGREEMENT WITH TENANT
- IS LEASE AGREEMENT SIGNED?
  - NO! → REVIEW TERMS WITH TENANT AND RENEGOTIATE
  - YES

6. MOVE-IN PROCESS
- COLLECT SECURITY DEPOSIT AND FIRST MONTH'S RENT
- CONDUCT PROPERTY WALK THROUGH WITH TENANT
- IS THE TENANT READY TO MOVE IN?
  - NO! → ADDRESS ISSUES BEFORE MOVE-IN
  - YES

7. ONGOING PROPERTY MANAGEMENT
- COLLECT RENT PAYMENTS MONTHLY
- RESPOND TO TENANT MAINTENANCE REQUESTS
- REGULAR PROPERTY INSPECTIONS
- ARE THERE ANY MAJOR ISSUES WITH THE PROPERTY?
  - NO! → CONTINUE PROPERTY MANAGEMENT AS USUAL
  - YES

8. MAINTENANCE & REPAIRS
- IDENTIFY AND PRIORITIZE REPAIRS
- HIRE CONTRACTORS OR HANDLE IN-HOUSE
- IS THE REPAIR COMPLETED?
  - NO! → RE-ASSESS TIMELINE AND MANAGE CONTRACTOR COMMUNICATION

CHAPTER 10
Scaling Your Portfolio

Once you've acquired and successfully managed your first investment, you can scale up to multiply your success.

1   **Leverage Equity:** Use equity from existing properties to finance or fund new purchases. Look at refinancing options to free up capital. Partner with other investors to increase buying power.

2   **Collaborative Strategies for Scaling:** Form partnerships with other investors to increase purchasing power, Syndication as a strategy to scale *(see Chapter 5)*, Joint ventures for sharing resources and minimizing individual risk.

3   **Leveraging Multiple Markets:** Diversify investments across different geographic locations, analyze emerging markets for high growth potential, Balance the advantages of local vs. out-of-state investments.

4   **Optimizing Your Portfolio for Scalability:** Sell underperforming properties to reinvest in high yield opportunities, refinance existing assets to free up equity, shift focus to property types with higher returns (e.g., multi-family, commercial).

5   **Embracing Technology for Growth:** Use analytics tools to evaluate property performance and market conditions, use automation in property management to handle multiple units efficiently, research online platforms for deal sourcing and tenant management.

6   **Mentoring and Networking for Growth:** Learn from seasoned investors who have successfully scaled their portfolios, join investor networks and mastermind groups for insights and opportunities, share your journey and experiences to build a supportive community.

SCALING YOUR PORTFOLIO

WHAT DO YOU WANT TO ACHIEVE?

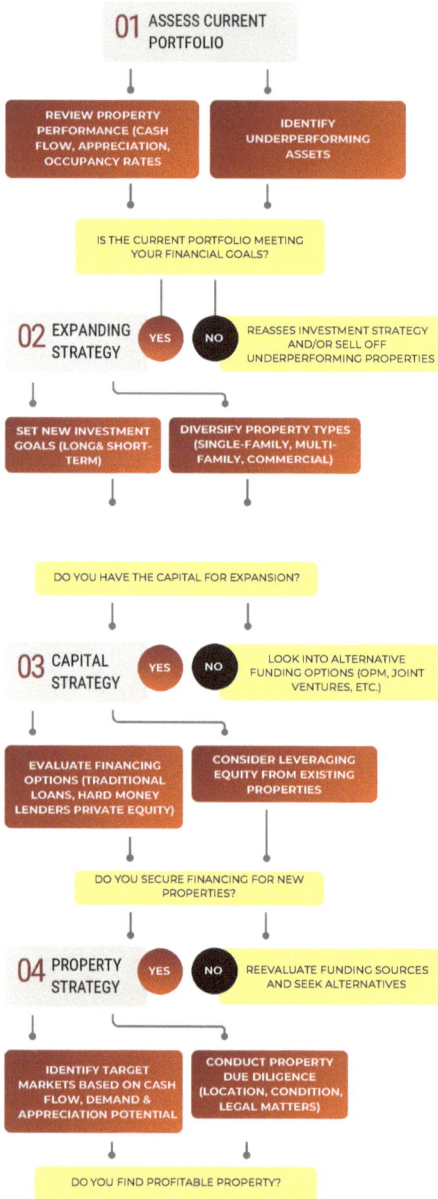

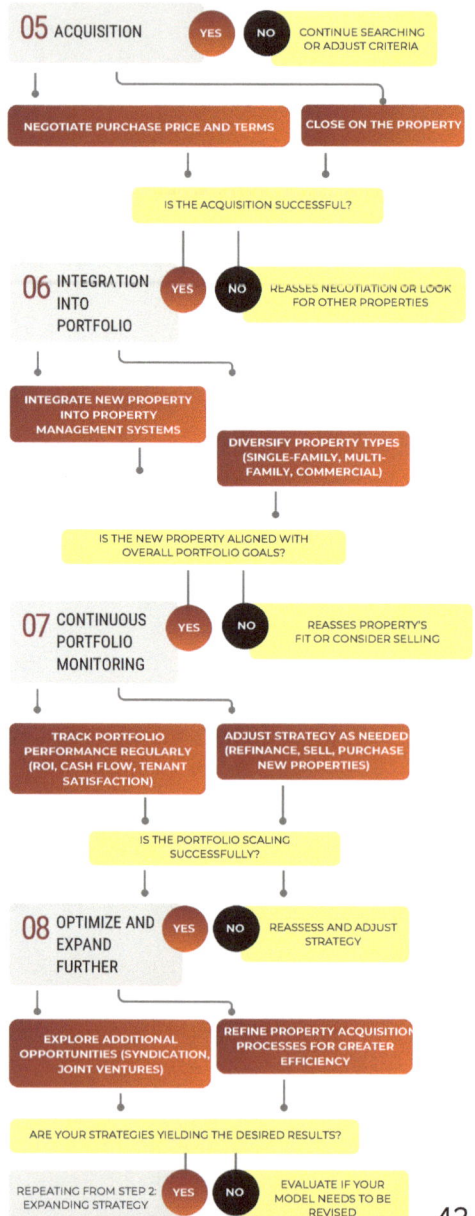

01 ASSESS CURRENT PORTFOLIO

REVIEW PROPERTY PERFORMANCE (CASH FLOW, APPRECIATION, OCCUPANCY RATES

IDENTIFY UNDERPERFORMING ASSETS

IS THE CURRENT PORTFOLIO MEETING YOUR FINANCIAL GOALS?

02 EXPANDING STRATEGY — YES / NO — REASSES INVESTMENT STRATEGY AND/OR SELL OFF UNDERPERFORMING PROPERTIES

SET NEW INVESTMENT GOALS (LONG& SHORT-TERM)

DIVERSIFY PROPERTY TYPES (SINGLE-FAMILY, MULTI-FAMILY, COMMERCIAL)

DO YOU HAVE THE CAPITAL FOR EXPANSION?

03 CAPITAL STRATEGY — YES / NO — LOOK INTO ALTERNATIVE FUNDING OPTIONS (OPM, JOINT VENTURES, ETC.)

EVALUATE FINANCING OPTIONS (TRADITIONAL LOANS, HARD MONEY LENDERS PRIVATE EQUITY)

CONSIDER LEVERAGING EQUITY FROM EXISTING PROPERTIES

DO YOU SECURE FINANCING FOR NEW PROPERTIES?

04 PROPERTY STRATEGY — YES / NO — REEVALUATE FUNDING SOURCES AND SEEK ALTERNATIVES

IDENTIFY TARGET MARKETS BASED ON CASH FLOW, DEMAND & APPRECIATION POTENTIAL

CONDUCT PROPERTY DUE DILIGENCE (LOCATION, CONDITION, LEGAL MATTERS)

DO YOU FIND PROFITABLE PROPERTY?

---

05 ACQUISITION — YES / NO — CONTINUE SEARCHING OR ADJUST CRITERIA

NEGOTIATE PURCHASE PRICE AND TERMS

CLOSE ON THE PROPERTY

IS THE ACQUISITION SUCCESSFUL?

06 INTEGRATION INTO PORTFOLIO — YES / NO — REASSES NEGOTIATION OR LOOK FOR OTHER PROPERTIES

INTEGRATE NEW PROPERTY INTO PROPERTY MANAGEMENT SYSTEMS

DIVERSIFY PROPERTY TYPES (SINGLE-FAMILY, MULTI-FAMILY, COMMERCIAL)

IS THE NEW PROPERTY ALIGNED WITH OVERALL PORTFOLIO GOALS?

07 CONTINUOUS PORTFOLIO MONITORING — YES / NO — REASSES PROPERTY'S FIT OR CONSIDER SELLING

TRACK PORTFOLIO PERFORMANCE REGULARLY (ROI, CASH FLOW, TENANT SATISFACTION)

ADJUST STRATEGY AS NEEDED (REFINANCE, SELL, PURCHASE NEW PROPERTIES)

IS THE PORTFOLIO SCALING SUCCESSFULLY?

08 OPTIMIZE AND EXPAND FURTHER — YES / NO — REASSESS AND ADJUST STRATEGY

EXPLORE ADDITIONAL OPPORTUNITIES (SYNDICATION, JOINT VENTURES)

REFINE PROPERTY ACQUISITION PROCESSES FOR GREATER EFFICIENCY

ARE YOUR STRATEGIES YIELDING THE DESIRED RESULTS?

REPEATING FROM STEP 2: EXPANDING STRATEGY — YES / NO — EVALUATE IF YOUR MODEL NEEDS TO BE REVISED

CHAPTER 11

Avoiding Common Pitfalls

Here are some mistakes new investors often make and how to avoid them:

1. **Overleveraging: Borrowing Too Much and Overextending Yourself Financially**

A common mistake new investors make is overleveraging or taking on more debt than they can reasonably manage. While leveraging allows you to purchase more properties or fund renovations, it also increases your financial risk. If market conditions shift or unexpected expenses arise, overleveraging can lead to cash flow issues, missed payments, or even foreclosure. To avoid this, carefully assess your debt-to-income ratio, ensure you have reserves for emergencies, and only borrow what you can comfortably repay even in worst-case scenarios. It's better to start small and scale sustainably than to risk losing it all.

2. **Poor Property Analysis: Not Accurately Calculating Costs and Returns**

Accurate property analysis is critical for making sound investment decisions. New investors often underestimate expenses such as closing costs, property taxes, insurance, and ongoing maintenance, leading to unanticipated financial strain. They may also overestimate rental income or appreciation potential, causing returns to fall short of expectations. Prevent this by thoroughly analyzing all potential costs and revenue streams using tools like cash flow calculators or spreadsheets. Always work with experienced professionals, such as real estate agents or real estate appraisers, to ensure the numbers align with your investment goals.

3. Ignoring Maintenance: Failing to Keep Up with Maintenance Can Lead to Costly Repairs Later

Neglecting maintenance can turn a profitable property into a money pit. Small issues, like leaky faucets or roof damage, can escalate into major repairs if it is left unaddressed. Not only does this increase costs, but it can also lead to tenant dissatisfaction and higher turnover. To avoid this, create a proactive maintenance plan that includes regular inspections, timely repairs, and a budget for ongoing upkeep. Building a network of reliable contractors and service providers can also help you address problems quickly and efficiently, preserving both the property's value and your bottom line.

4. Underestimating Time and Effort: Real Estate Investing Can Be Demanding; Plan Accordingly

Many new investors underestimate the time, effort, and skills required to succeed in real estate investing. From researching properties and managing tenants to navigating legal and financial complexities, the workload can be significant. Treat your investments as a business and approach each task with the necessary dedication. Create a schedule to manage your responsibilities and consider outsourcing time-intensive tasks, like property management, if it aligns with your budget. Planning and setting realistic expectations can help you maintain balance while growing your portfolio.

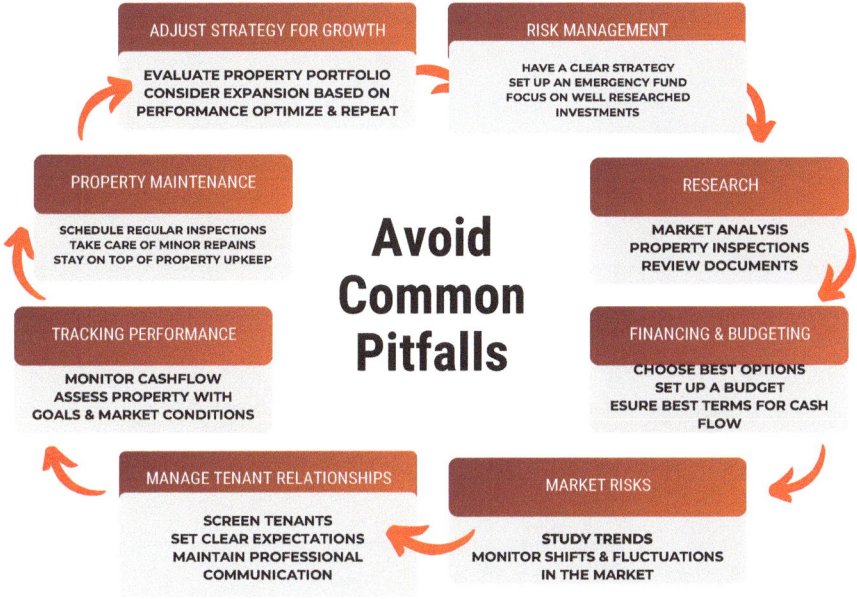

ADJUST STRATEGY FOR GROWTH

EVALUATE PROPERTY PORTFOLIO
CONSIDER EXPANSION BASED ON
PERFORMANCE OPTIMIZE & REPEAT

RISK MANAGEMENT

HAVE A CLEAR STRATEGY
SET UP AN EMERGENCY FUND
FOCUS ON WELL RESEARCHED
INVESTMENTS

PROPERTY MAINTENANCE

SCHEDULE REGULAR INSPECTIONS
TAKE CARE OF MINOR REPAINS
STAY ON TOP OF PROPERTY UPKEEP

RESEARCH

MARKET ANALYSIS
PROPERTY INSPECTIONS
REVIEW DOCUMENTS

**Avoid
Common
Pitfalls**

TRACKING PERFORMANCE

MONITOR CASHFLOW
ASSESS PROPERTY WITH
GOALS & MARKET CONDITIONS

FINANCING & BUDGETING

CHOOSE BEST OPTIONS
SET UP A BUDGET
ESURE BEST TERMS FOR CASH
FLOW

MANAGE TENANT RELATIONSHIPS

SCREEN TENANTS
SET CLEAR EXPECTATIONS
MAINTAIN PROFESSIONAL
COMMUNICATION

MARKET RISKS

STUDY TRENDS
MONITOR SHIFTS & FLUCTUATIONS
IN THE MARKET

45

AVOID COMMON PITFALLS

IDENTIFY POTENTIAL MISTAKES

- **LACK OF RESEARCH**
- **OVERLEVERAGING**
- **IGNORING DUE DILIGENCE**

⭐ ⭐ ⭐ ⭐ ⭐

RISK MANAGEMENT STRATEGY

- Develop a clear investment strategy based on your goals, timeline, and risk tolerance
- Create an emergency fund for unexpected expenses or market downturns
- Mitigate risks by focusing on long-term, well-researched investments

FINANCING & BUDGETING

- Choose the best financing options suited to your investment strategy (traditional loans, hard money. seller financing
- Prepare a realistic budget, accounting for a acquisition. renovation, and ongoing operational costs
- Ensure financial terms align with your cash flow goals

ADJUST STRATEGY FOR GROWTH

- Continuously evaluate your property portfolio and investment goals
- Consider expanding or divesting based on performance and market shifts
- Optimize your strategy to scale your portfolio while mitigating risks

RESEARCH

- Conduct thorough market analysis to assess location market trends, and potential for growth
- Perform detailed property inspections to identify structural issues, repairs. of hidden costs
- Review title and legal documents for any zoning or permit issues

MARKET RISKS

- Study local market trends, including supply and demand, rental rates, and economic indicators
- Account for long-term market fluctuations, including property values and interest rates
- Monitor shifts in the market that could affect your investments' profitability

TRACKING PERFORMANCE

- Regularly monitor key performance metrics such as cash flow, ROI occupancy rates, and appreciation
- Assess how the property is performing against your investment goals and market conditions

PROPERTY MAINTENANCE

- Schedule regular property inspections to prevent costly repairs
- Address minor repairs early to avoid escalation into major issues
- Keep up with necessary property upkeep to maintain its value and avoid costly fixes later

CHAPTER 12

Final Tips for Success

> **Start Small:** Focus on smaller, TINY, and more manageable investments before scaling up.
> **Learn Continuously:** Stay updated on market trends and investment strategies.
> **Build Relationships:** Networking is key to finding deals and growing your business.

Real estate investing is a journey. To succeed, it's crucial to combine a strong foundation with continuous growth, adaptability, and a focus on long-term goals.

1. Aligning Personal Goals with Investment Strategies

A key principle of successful real estate investing is ensuring your investments align with your personal goals.

Are you aiming for financial independence, a steady cash flow, or long-term wealth building?

Different goals require a different strategy.

When your personal goals are in sync with your strategies, you stay motivated and focused. For instance, if your goal is to retire early, prioritizing passive income properties may be the right path. Alternatively, if you thrive on creative projects, flipping houses or developing properties could be more fulfilling. By aligning these two aspects, you're not just chasing profits - you're building a future that matches your vision.

2. Building and Sustaining Relationships

Real estate is a people-centered business. The relationships you build with your team, mentors, tenants, and other investors can significantly impact your success.

- **Nurture Existing Connections:** Regularly follow up with your team, such as property managers, realtors, and contractors. Express gratitude and acknowledge their contributions.
- **Expand Your Network:** Attend real estate meetups, conferences, and online forums to meet like minded investors and industry experts.
- **Provide Value to Others:** Offer your expertise or share opportunities with your network without expecting anything in return. Relationships thrive when built on mutual trust and benefit.

Strong relationships lead to smoother deals, insider market knowledge, and even off-market opportunities.

3. Staying Disciplined and Organized

Discipline and organization are a MUST for successful investing.

- **Time Management:** Set aside dedicated time each week to manage your properties, research new deals, or educate yourself.

- **Record-Keeping:** Maintain detailed records of your properties, expenses, and income. Using tools like property management software or financial tracking apps can save you time and stress.

- **Consistent Review:** Regularly review your portfolio's performance and adjust as needed.

An organized approach not only minimizes stress but also positions you to act quickly when new opportunities arise.

4. The Importance of Education

The real estate market is constantly evolving, stay ahead by committing to lifelong learning:

- Read books, blogs, and market reports.
- Attend seminars, workshops, and online courses.
- Join professional organizations like the National Association of Realtors (NAR) or a Real Estate Investors Association (REIA), local investment clubs.

Educated investors are better equipped to identify profitable deals, navigate market changes, and avoid costly mistakes.

5. **Keep a Growth-Oriented Mindset**

Success in Real Estate often hinges on your mindset. Challenges such as a market downturn, unexpected expenses, or a bad tenant experience are inevitable, but how you respond makes all the difference.

> Stay Positive: Focus on solutions rather than dwelling on problems.

> **Embrace Failure:** Treat setbacks as learning opportunities. Each mistake can refine your approach and make you a stronger investor.

> **Celebrate Wins:** Acknowledge your achievements, no matter how small, to keep your momentum and motivation high.

A growth-oriented mindset keeps you adaptable and open to new opportunities.

6. **Giving Back to the Community**

Real estate investors have the power to create a positive impact in their communities.

> Invest in properties that uplift neighborhoods, such as affordable housing or revitalization projects.

> Mentor aspiring investors who are just starting out.

> Partner with local charities or sponsor community events.

When you give back, you not only improve the lives of others but also build goodwill, trust, and a reputation as a responsible business.

7. **Action Plan for Continued Success**

To maintain momentum after completing this book, take the following steps:

> **Set Clear Goals:** Outline your short term and long term objectives. Revisit these goals annually to ensure they remain relevant.

> **Create a Strategy:** Develop a concrete plan based on the investment approaches discussed in this guide.

> **Take Action:** Start small but start NOW. Whether it's analyzing a deal, joining a real estate group, or buying your first property, taking action is the first step toward success.

For your free bonus action plan go to:
https://www.elpasoinvestorsclub.com/burn_your_9-5_take_action_plan

Analysis paralysis is a common pitfall for beginners. Start where you are with what you have and build from there.

Real estate investing has the potential to transform your financial future and your life. It requires careful planning and commitment.

By following these steps, setting clear goals, and continuously educating yourself, you can set yourself up for long-term success.

FINAL TIPS FOR SUCCESS

Aligning personal goals with investment strategies will help you stay focused, make informed decisions, and achieve both financial success and personal fulfillment in your real estate business.

START SMALL

SET REALISTIC, ACTIONABLE SHORT-TERM AND LONG-TERM GOALS.
FOCUS ON WHAT'S MANAGEABLE FOR YOU BEFORE SCALING UP.

STAY GROWTH ORIENTED

EMBRACE CHALLENGES AS OPPORTUNITIES.
STAY POSITIVE AND RESILIENT THROUGH MARKET FLUCTUATIONS.
CELEBRATE SMALL WINS TO STAY MOTIVATED.

SET YOUR PRIORITIES

USE TOOLS AND SYSTEMS TO STAY ON TOP OF TASKS, DEADLINES, AND FINANCES.
AVOID COMMON PITFALLS OF PROCRASTINATION OR OVERCOMMITMENT.

NETWORKING

STRONG RELATIONSHIPS CAN OPEN DOORS TO NEW OPPORTUNITIES.
SHOW GRATITUDE AND KEEP IN TOUCH WITH YOUR CONNECTIONS.

GIVE BACK

INVEST IN WAYS THAT POSITIVELY IMPACT YOUR LOCAL COMMUNITY.
MENTOR NEW INVESTORS OR SHARE KNOWLEDGE WITH PEERS.

Your business will be built on persistence, knowledge, and the relationships you cultivate.

If you're ready to dive deeper, consider exploring more advanced strategies, connecting with experienced investors, or seeking mentorship.

https://www.elpasoinvestorsclub.com/

Best Success-

Lacy O'Leary